Sea Fever

DALE FRANZEN

Illustrated by Don Erik Franzen using his Apple Pencil

I dedicate this tiny tome to my father
who loved the poem Sea Fever as I do!
And to my husband of many years
who has supported me in all my fevers!

I must go down to the seas again, to the lonely sea and the sky,
And all I ask is a tall ship and a star to steer her by;
And the wheel's kick and the wind's song and the white sail's shaking,
And a grey mist on the sea's face, and a grey dawn breaking.

I must go down to the seas again, for the call of the running tide
Is a wild call and a clear call that may not be denied;
And all I ask is a windy day with the white clouds flying,
And the flung spray and the blown spume, and the sea-gulls crying.

I must go down to the seas again, to the vagrant gypsy life,
To the gull's way and the whale's way where the winds like a whetted knife;
And all I ask is a merry yarn from a laughing fellow-rover,
And quiet sleep and a sweet dream when the long trick's over.

Sea Fever
By John Masefield

Preface

I almost drowned when I was eight years old. The whole time I was in mortal danger, what I remember clearly is not that I was about to crash into the rocks, but that I was singing to the mermaids in the sea.

Moments after I was rescued by three men and taken safely to shore, I asked my mom if I could go back in the ocean. Needless to say, the answer was "No."

This morning I woke up thinking about my deep, lifelong love of the sea and other natural bodies of water, and how happy I am when immersed in their depths, or just gazing at or listening to the ocean.

I never feel happier, safer, or freer than when I am in the water. It cleanses me, enchants me, makes me feel like an adventurer. And for those minutes or hours I can think about nothing but the water. I am cast into another world where I am a small player who becomes one with the greater, mysterious universe of water.

The water is alive, pulsing, and always different. And I am always different in it.

Starting a few years ago, I felt a great and deep need to get back into the water, and so I started swimming in the Pacific Ocean, right near my house, and swam all through the winter months of Southern California.

If you read the ocean weather reports, as soon as the water drops to 62 degrees, they declare it "TOO COLD FOR SWIMMING." This year my open water swim teacher and I swam with water temperatures as high as 74 degrees, down to 56 degrees at its coldest, and loved it! For serious cold water and open water swimmers, this is not even considered very cold. Ask any UK or Scandinavian swimmers!

The last year of pandemic lockdown, which even included several weeks of beach and ocean lockdown, have been hard on everyone. I had a bad case of Sea Fever. What that helped me to realize is that we all have to find something that brings us moments of joy, of repose, of peace, of silence, of freedom, and of adventure that lifts our spirits out of the everyday trauma of this world right now.

This, of course, comes in many forms and we must each discover our own. Be it yoga, T'ai chi, meditation, gardening, religion, painting, cooking, baking bread, crafting, napping, working on environmental causes, advocating voter registration, fighting for racial equity, writing poetry, making music, hiking, dancing, learning something new, enjoying a good read or movie, calling friends, or maybe even a combination of all of the above —the possibilities are endless. We must find a place to feel safe and nourished, trusting we can survive the global fear, anxiety, and trauma that has been unleashed on us all, and may not end any time soon.

There's only one way through this, and that is to find what gives you a beneficial break from reality so that you can rest your mind, body, and soul, and keep yourself replenished and healthy.

We are at war and all we can do is stay present and persevere and fight however we can each day.

So, I decided to write this little book and share how I got through 2020.

Sea Fever

The Beach as a Democratic Metaphor

I have been a Southern California ocean swimmer for quite a while, and a lifetime believer in the healing and restorative power of the sea. During COVID-19, all this became even more precious and important to me, especially when my local beach was literally shut down. I felt the heartbreak of being barred from my favorite place and, more importantly, of not being able to take in and absorb the healing magic of the ocean, either in or out of it. For me, the majestic blue-green ocean is the only place where I feel truly and completely safe, happy, and free of worry.

When you swim in the Pacific Ocean, folks, you often have the entire ocean to yourself. This is real "social distancing" — still possible even in a city of 10 million people like Los Angeles.

This tiny book is about the daily adventures I had while swimming in the ocean, walking, meditating, and gazing at the beach. I've come to realize that democracy works best when we are all united in an experience. The ocean beaches are open and available to everyone, and offer a truly democratic experience. Big or small, any and all colors, sizes, nationalities, languages, and beliefs — we can all meet there and enjoy the possibilities of a shared, sensual experience of engaging with the natural world and feeling hopeful and free.

Here are a few tiny stories about the folks I met at the beach....

Today

Gorgeous man dancing in the sand for his girlfriend as she videotaped him. I smiled and said, "How about you both dance and I'll film you?" They beamed excitedly and handed me the camera. I proceeded to create a spontaneous Hollywood 360-degree panoramic dance video! The whole thing lasted three minutes and we were all laughing as we parted.

Another Day

Walking, I pass a couple (in their late seventies, I'm guessing) playing bad-
minton, smiling, and laughing. I smile back and the man says to me in a thick
French accent, "Today we want to do EVERYTHING!" I laugh and nod, understanding their desire completely.

Tomorrow is so uncertain

Morning Swim

A young woman asks if she can swim in the ocean with me. I say, "Of course!"
This lovely lady, I discover, is a former personal assistant to a major Hollywood
A-List film actress. Now she owns and operates a mobile in-home organic spray
tanning business. *Only in Malibu!* I chuckle to myself.

Afternoon Delight

Today the ocean is wild.
The waves are strong and fearsome.
Dare I go in or not?

Smiles and Mangos

Today everyone seems cautious and sleepy. Lots of folks are reading or just staring at the ocean. A man selling fresh mango slices passes by and we share a smile. I don't go in today – it's just — too rough.

Early Morning Walk

Walking the shore in the morning mist, the dolphins follow along with me.
We are all so deeply connected – whether we know it or not.
Later, two seagulls flying together in perfectly syncopated harmony, skimming the waves.
I wonder, are they lovers or just friends?

Walking

I pass two happy lovers enjoying the sunset while drinking a cheery toast in the back seat of their parked car. I was so touched by their romantic interlude that I offered to take their photo. Immediately they lurched apart and shouted, "No! No! No!" I was momentarily startled, and then I blurted out, "Oh! You're having an affair!" They both grinned with guilty pleasure. I walked on thinking about how many secrets and stories there are at the beach.

Swim

Today was glorious and sunny.
A perfect California beach boy day.
I am swimming and smiling.

A cheerful male swimmer comes by and says, "Such a perfect day! Paradise." We have the 'typical swimmer chat' about how lucky we are, how calm the waves are today, how the water is the perfect temperature for swimming... It turns out that he is one of my local lifeguards and has been doing this for thirty years.

After Qi Gong Today

A vibrant, colorfully dressed woman walks by with her Caribbean music blasting. It was some kind of funky dance melody. We stop and share a smiley improv dance.

Beach Walk

End of May, a few days after George Floyd was murdered in Minneapolis, a serious-looking middle-aged Black man is walking toward me on the path. "How are you doing?" I ask him. He stops, pauses, then tells me that his faith is helping him get through this, but it's a very sad and difficult time. We talk for a little while, listening and sharing feelings, two total strangers at the beach. Then we nod and move on.

Not for the first time, I think, "I wish I had faith like that." I often wonder if the practical good of religious faith is that it is there for those who need its comfort most: those who have been mistreated and suffer unjustly at the hands of society.

Silent Swim

Since the pandemic began I have gradually become less and less talkative, seeking and enjoying both inner and outer silence. It's as though both my brain and my soul need to rest in the quiet and in nature more than ever. There is no silence like the silence of swimming solo. Time spent propelling oneself through the water is all about gliding, kicking, inhaling, exhaling—the essentials. No time even for thoughts, other than noticing if the sky is clear or cloudy, or the waves are rolling or calm, or if there's a fish or seal or surfer nearby. Silence is needed more now in order to absorb the trauma of our daily life and times. We need it to contain our confusion and despair, as well as our hope, and to feed our strength to recover and just keep going.

Today with My Seal Friend

Two marine mammals in motion – both of us take the rolling waves eagerly, aware of the other's presence, giving each other plenty of room to glide along and fully enjoy this perfect, sunlit day. You never know, while out among the waves, who your next companion might be.

Beach Bum

My father always told me that he would live out the end of his life as a happy beach bum — unshaven and suntanned.
He died too soon – too young to live out this idyllic dream.
Will I fulfill his prophecy?

Today After My Swim

Sitting in my garden, a West Coast housewife doing laundry, cooking and cleaning. I am amazed at how little I want to speak to anyone. It feels so hard and requires so much energy. We are all waiting for the election in a state of anguish.

What's Next?

I am headed to Big Island, Hawaii. I have found a gorgeous 20-acre rural plot of tropical paradise with a panoramic view of the Pacific Ocean — and its own waterfall!

How will living in that exotic, sea-rimmed nature change me? I wonder.

Will it help me to focus, clarify, and concentrate?

I am in a state of pause.

I have cleared my decks and await direction.

What next does this life offer or require of me?

Maybe to tend the land with my girls, or perhaps just to *be*, aimless and contented, till the next enlightening idea strikes.

I have faith that it will reveal itself – as it always has – when this madness frees my mind.

Arriving on the Big Island of Hawaii

Today I'm staring at the wild surf along the most beautiful beach in the world, just below my rental house. Perfection, Hapuna! After lunch, I venture down and take a dip in the refreshing, pristine river off the wave break.

I am in Hawaii. A lean, leather-skinned, older Haole woman waves and says, "Hey – Don't I know you?" "I guess we're just sisters," I respond, and we hug, unafraid of disease – or of anything life-threatening – in this moment. Here on the Island, we trust.

Second Day Hilo Heaven

I spent the day walking along the splendid shores of lush green gorgeous rain forest. I ended the day boogie-boarding with my daughter and feeling the Mainland drifting farther and farther away with all its madness.

Here we need less...yet nature gives us more.

Later

Today I woke up overcome with sadness and a feeling of disconnect. Even when I am right up against the rolling waves I still feel I'm not close enough. Can we ever get close enough?

I feel extremely guilty about hiding away on this island, but I also feel I'm in preparation for something new. I'm not sure what will be revealed or when, but my friends and family say I deserve this extended retreat to recover from the last several crazy, busy years. And don't we all deserve this?

In the meantime, I'm listening to a musician friend's new album, thrilled to know there are still so many good people out there creating and working in the real world while I lay low for a while on this island, warmly held and generously fed by Mother Nature.

Rainy Morning

Ahhhh, the heavens have given us rain today. I didn't realize how much I missed its sound, moisture, and gift. Coming from a dry, fire prone and water challenged state, this feels like heaven. The surfers are still out as raindrops splatter the waves.

I just read the following words of Dan Fawkes, a long-serving lifeguard, and think this is true of any body of water. A recurring theme is the equalizing nature of the ponds. He talks of "the different characters I meet, who I wouldn't normally rub shoulders with." He adds, "Once you're in the pond together, it doesn't matter what background you're from or how well you've done in life."

Again, I see how democracy is at work in the waves.

Another Day

Watching the very serious faces of two seven-year-olds on the beach building elaborate sand castles. No smiles, just the hard work of play, and increasing pride in their citadels of sand. No matter their crumbly creations will soon be flooded and destroyed by the incoming tide...

Motto

"If in doubt, stay out (side)" is my new motto. If you aren't clear of your intentions, stay put. Pause. Do nothing, actively. Wait for a direction that is clear and steady.

Swimming Kona Side Afternoon

Water like a bath,
Clear as crystal,
White sand.
A real vacation postcard.
And not very many people know about
This secluded beach – It's an easy hike.
Paradise.

Today at 9 a.m.

Richardson beach.
Wavy, curly waves.
Real body.
I go out for a short swim and see lots of older sea swimmers.
May join their group?
They are friendly, helpful, and want everyone to feel welcome and safe.
Every day is a different ocean,
I get a little bit closer.

October Morning Hawaii

Swimming in the gorgeous warm water today with my daughter boogie board-ing nearby. I head out with goggles and fins, so that I am neither snorkeling nor swimming, but "sea hiking", as my new swim partner, Steve, says.

We meet in the waves far from shore, as swimmers do, and have a friendly conversation. He invites me to follow him through a lovely passage. Along the way we come upon a spectacular view of colorful fish and rolling waves. This must be Heaven. Everything is right with the world and comes into balance in the water.

It is a joy that is hard to explain. Time expands in nature. What I can say is that the world can appear to be a chaotic mess, but when you're swimming you become part of an alternate universe. You are a small stranger visiting a great mysterious kingdom.

Back home now in my country cottage—spent and weary. This is a different world – quiet and still and dry. Yet the distant rolling ocean beckons, and – as relentlessly as waves slapping the shore – it pulls me back each day for more.

Song

"Listen to me.
The human world, it's a mess.
Life under the sea is better than anything
they've got up there."

-Alan Menken and Howard Ashman from
Disney's The Little Mermaid

Big I Hawaii

A few months into my sojourning sheltering here I see two large bright green geckos energetically mating on my bedroom wall. I don't even blink, as this is a daily natural occurrence. How simply one can adapt — we humans and we animals. If I don't swim each day now, I feel sad and out of sorts, as if the ocean saltwater were life itself. Which, of course, it is.

Dawn Pre-Swim Upcountry

What I love about this island is the absolute quiet.
All I can hear is the wind through the trees.
I even think I hear clouds moving overhead.
Watching the sun rise over the vast blue.
Remarkable.

Thoughts Today

Just as the theater, in which I have spent my life, is a transcendent experience, so too is the ocean. The ocean is its own kind of theater, and it is definitely transcendent. A new cast and a different performance each day. Never the same show, that's for sure.

Also —

There's something about islands surrounded by water. Rushing just doesn't seem necessary, or even possible here, as there always seems to be an abundance of time.

I just watched the Oscar-winning documentary, *My Octopus Teacher*. Wild! I get it!

Hawaiians believe you *keep pono* with the land and people. To be pono means to be in a state of harmony and balance with oneself, others, the land, work, and life itself. So in this spirit, rather than asking for something, you wait to receive.

You will often see whole groups of Hawaiians or locals just sitting together in the water, quietly observing, absorbing. They don't effort or move, but remain receptive, allowing the water to move and shift them around. Something I am pondering and appreciating more each day.

Relaxing today after a good swim—how I feel no rush and no pressure. I feel, for the first time in years, that I have all the time in the world. The island stretches out time for me. And yes, it bends where I want it. I have days to wonder and wander as I like, and each day will show me the water in some way.

It's Fine for Me

There are signs everywhere that say, "STAY OUT! STRONG CURRENTS!" but the lifeguards tell me the warnings are for the tourists who don't know how to swim and it's fine for me to go out. "You're a strong swimmer!" The lifeguard tells me how pleasurable the pandemic has been for him personally: watching over beautiful empty beaches with no at-risk tourists for the first time in his life. Heaven.

Island Ramblings

At home, I always feel I must make things happen.

Here—I relax and let things happen.

I have a feeling that all will be revealed, discovered, and I am not in a rush.

Sunday Rest and Reading

Just read an interesting piece written by the great Spanish-Puerto Rican cellist, Pablo Casals:

"I do not think a day passes in my life in which I fail to look with fresh amazement at the miracle of nature. It is there on every side. I have always especially loved the sea. Whenever possible, I have lived by the sea... It has long been a custom of mine to walk along the beach each morning before I start to work. True, my walks are shorter than they used to be, but that does not lessen the wonder of the sea. How mysterious and beautiful is the sea! How infinitely variable! It is never the same, never, not from one moment to the next, always in the process of change, always becoming something different and new."

Sunrise October

In Hawaii, on this island, I have become a morning person, because who would want to miss the glorious sunrise here that pulls you to her shores? I want to wake up somewhere where there is no killing drought, no forest fires, and there's always plenty of water.

Fearless and Sturdy

Dark, stormy island skies, but I go in anyway. The ocean is a roller coaster, but a few intrepid swimmers are out — and of course so are the fishes! I swim for a while, the water warm and cozy, but after a few sizeable sets I head back in. Healthy caution is wise in unfamiliar seas where you don't know the characteristic currents or rips. As I'm leaving I see a deeply tanned woman, much older than me, heading straight out into the turbulent, rocky waves. She's a local, no doubt — fearless and sturdy. I will get there one day.

Later

Is my desire to be on the sea a metaphor for surrender, which is what this year has asked of me? Each day I surrender to the waves, however big or unpredictable, to see how it feels and how I do. I surrender. That is what this year is all about. I must change and grow and develop, and the first step is to surrender fully, unconditionally, to the open wave, so I can move forward and see what comes next.

Wild at Heart

Just saw this homemade sign on a tree trunk at the beach!

And aren't we all looking to become more primitive – more wild and free? The sun is shining brightly today and I head out beyond the breakers. I meet up with the same staunch group of swimmers and decide to go out with them this Sunday, come hell or high water. (Pun intended.)

The swimmers are friendly and unpretentious. The conversation is easy and this feels like a fun outing, rather than a competitive marathon race. Though I am not a group person, I am going to try and see if I can push myself a bit more and keep up with the gang. In any case, it's safer to learn to navigate unfamiliar sets of waves with those who've gone before you.

Gratitude

"Aue, aue
We keep our island in our mind
And when it's time to find home
We know the way"

-Lin-Manuel Miranda, Mark Mancina, and Opetaia Foa'i from Disney's *Moana*

Dancing to the music of Moana with my lovely island daughters. Gratitude to Moana and her love of the water!

Today

I had a spur-of-the-moment swim with my eldest daughter who, for the past several years, has made this island her home. How wonderful to reside in the same small island town and be able to be spontaneous together, for the first time ever, as adults! It is a profound switch from the previous scenario of the roving daughter returning home to her parents' house, to the parents now visiting and experiencing their daughter in her uniquely bold and imaginative life!

The lifeguard tells me the winter swell has come and the current is rough on this side of the island. Never turn your back on the ocean! I go in cautiously.

Another Day

One of the true delights of daily life here is seeing the massive humpback whales breaching out at sea. Between mid-December and mid-April over 10,000 humpbacks migrate from their summer feeding grounds in Alaska. Every winter, thousands of humpback whales travel to the warm, shallow waters of Hawaii to mate, give birth, and raise their young.

The people who live on these islands boast a rich mixture of skin colors, but the white-skinned Haoles (non-native foreigners) are the intruders.

The term 'Haole' became popular during the 1820s and was used to describe European immigrants who came to Hawaii during that time. One lingering theory is that "haole" meant "no breath." In Polynesian culture, people traditionally inhale and share in each other's breath when they first meet. Foreigners did not partake of this custom. When Captain Cook arrived on the island, many Hawaiians believed that he and his non-native men did not have any breath, which explained why they were so white – hence the origin of the "no breath" definition.

These days so many Haoles, especially in America, are working on developing their breath and improving their breathing techniques.

The idea of *Pono* (righteousness with each other, with our land) is the philosophy Hawaii wants to reclaim. But it's hard when so many Haoles who come here just want to replicate their lives on the mainland without regard for the damage they do. As usual, I don't feel I fit in or identify with the Haoles, even though I am one, but I also recognize that I'm an outsider to the natives, for whom I have the deepest gratitude and respect. I can only do my best to appreciate and honor their native wisdom traditions and culture.

Thoughts Before November 3

I have huge moments of losing faith in the human race. Deep sadness in our continued history of neglect, hate, and violence. I see no end in sight. Just another swing toward justice, but will that just swing back again? But then I feel hopeful and positive the next moment when I see nature here in all its splendor.

A dizzying yo-yo mind these pandemic days...

Election Swim

I haven't slept much lately and my stomach is full of unease. I have been thinking about compassion and understanding and how I just may have to exercise those muscles if my team doesn't win tomorrow. The last hundred years have seen great progress, and at least, as American political activist Jodie Evans says, "Even if we lose, more folks know the truth now." Meanwhile, today I swim in the warm clear waters of Puako. I find an empty mind for a little while and a nudist beach behind a cove. This reminds me that you never know what's just around the next curve – so keep going, and keep swimming!

Election Still Not Resolved – November 4

Feel absolutely shattered and can't stop crying. So I just stay still at home and listen to the waves crashing. "This is just today" is my mantra.

Where Do I Belong?

Late Morning. I am watching Hawaiian sea turtles poke their heads up and wave. I feel homeless, as if I no longer belong in my own home, but also, clearly don't belong anywhere else. Nowhere is safe. It just feels safer here. After all the cycles of life I have been through, here is my new one. I'm not sure where I'm supposed to nest. Maybe the whole planet feels unhoused and uprooted right now.

Later

Nothing to do but go for a good swim and let go of the machinations of human folly for a bit. The ocean is beautiful, the waves a bit rocky, so an invigorating swim takes my full attention. I am on the lookout for sudden swells of waves. My heart is pounding and muscles are working.

My mantra is *I am here*. I am here, with the ocean, and we are constant and in a constant state of change.

Friday – and Still No President

What a week—I've been up, down, and all around, as has everyone I know. Today, after a stormy, windy night, hearing the ocean and feeling the wind, I am taking a slow morning and just watching the sea. Imagining myself gliding like a seal, diving deep and having endless breath. Later I'll go for a swim and try this out.

November 8, 2020

Today is the start of a new week, a new American President and administration, and a new hope. Like the waves, every day will be different, but it feels like we can all take a deep breath of welcome relief, purpose, and positive transition.

Today, I am at the sea. The wind and waves are particularly strong today, as if to say: *Come in. Don't be scared. We got this. Take precautions but go forth.* And so, I do.

Back From Swim

Sky, overcast.
Water high and rolling wildly.
"We don't turn our backs on the sea, and we work with what we have,"
say the Hawaiians.
That's good life advice.
You are not alone.
Together we save each other.
Joe and Kamala. And us.
We got this *together*.

This year has propelled many of us to contemplate and pay attention to our internal voices – our *gnosis*. Personal transformation comes in waves, and you don't always know where you're headed. You have to investigate, but also have faith that all will be revealed if you stay open to opportunity and to your soul's messages. The ocean has helped me so much to do that this year.

Afternoon

Watching the wild and crazy northern swell. I see some fun things.

A young man leans over and kisses his girlfriend's bronzed buttocks, exposed by her thong bathing suit. Sweet...!

Another young man (he tells me he's from Louisiana) rocks in his own private hammock, reading a good book that his grandma recommended.

I follow an elder female swimmer in a red bathing suit as she strokes gracefully back and forth in this big tide and strong current.

A little way out to sea a big volcanic rock with two young lovers perched on it, watching the break.

If you slow down and look, there is much wonderment and beauty to see on this Planet Earth. Today I can't stop smiling. *Ahhhhhhh!*

Drunkard

Today the waves are high and rolling like a drunkard and I am like a drunkard bouncing around inside them. They're moved by the winds and current at different speeds. A fast, windblown swim today, and then suddenly I'm on shore with the sand beneath me. I walk out, still feeling off-balance. Laughing like a drunk and realizing we are all off-kilter, but still moving forward.

Maybe maintaining one's balance is overrated? Better to be able to move through imbalance and stay upright? Go with the waves. Go with the currents. Don't fight it. Conserve energy. Wait for the next shift in the current, the next variation of wave.

Winter Solstice

The Great Conjunction. Sometimes the elements speak too loudly to be ignored. Last night the earth, in the form of hot molten lava, spewed forth from Kīlauea, the youngest and most active of the five volcanoes that together form the Big Island of Hawaii. Traditionally, Kīlauea is the home of the powerful volcanic deity, Pelehonuamea (Pele).

According to ancient Hawaiian chants, the revered goddess Pele's function is creating new land, but also destroying what was once there. She is both destructive and creative in nature. In Hawaiian tradition, it is customary to ask permission from Pele to travel through her land and this sacred landscape.

Last night the ocean's mountains shifted and erupted. The heavens poured rain and the stars aligned in new ways. Since then I find I can't sleep. Listening. Waiting. Passions driving the very planet. Asking, wondering...what's next?

Whoosh and Whirling

We are definitely out of control, or perhaps never had any to begin with, but now we are paying attention. The storm is over. The golden Hawaiian sun shines down and the sapphire waters are crystal clear. Jeweled fishes abound and I propel my arms and legs to swim with them. I'm trying to learn their ways of ease and glide. The ocean never ceases to amaze me. There is such a treasure of abundance within the mystery.

A New Day

A big-eyed local seven-year-old boy chats with me so earnestly. He knows nothing of the trouble the planet is in. He just wants to know what fishes I saw today.

The Holidays

Lovely meal and Christmastime with my beautiful family, but I'm feeling down. My husband says I get sad at holidays. Really? Why? Is it the primitive feeling of missing my original family? I've been thinking how I wished I had been kinder to and more sympathetic toward my mom, and that I had much more time with my dad. I have all the questions that I will never know the answers to. Now I am old and wonder—why should this even matter?

Later

Lovely family time with the girls today. They are grown-ups and so funny and original. I am always learning more about them, as they reveal and unveil their grown women selves. It is beautiful to watch. It's a blessed time here on this island with my children so close. I feel like I am slipping into a new reality. We are pivoting, adjusting, living more presently, slowing down, pausing and taking time to reflect. The end of this terrible year is finally upon us.

Reserves

Today's swim was so hard. I had so little energy, but I kept going as long as I could. I still felt safe and that I had enough strength and stamina left in reserve in case it became difficult getting back to shore. You always have to gauge the wind and sea currents, as well as your own energy, in order to anticipate how hard the return trip will be.

Birds

I am listening to the tropical birds sing to each other and wonder, "What the hell are they saying?" I find the choral repetition soothing, the sing-song sounds. Sometimes it feels as if the island is breathing, the earth vibrating, and – well, yes, it is. But now I can actually tune in and hear it...

Late January

Today I'm watching tons of Hawaiian green sea turtles (honu) swimming in the shallow waters and sunbathing on the volcanic rock outcroppings. I am thinking of these turtles and what we can learn from them. They have traveled thousands of miles through strong ocean currents with terrible eyesight. Although they can remain resting underwater for several hours, while traveling they need to surface every few minutes to get oxygen into their lungs. And then, months later, they travel back, mysteriously, to their same nesting place. Scientists can't figure this out. Is it just going with the flow?

Another Night and Day

My husband has taken to going topless all the time. He hasn't worn a shirt in months now. Here on this island, we both want to get as close to nature and the elements as possible. Go native. Go natural. Let Go.

Water Dragon

Musing today, as it is Chinese New Year. I was born in the Year of the Water Dragon.

Today at Hapuna

Overheard. Made me smile.
Very sunny day—80 degrees.
A local woman says to her mate, "It's so cold today and the water's freezing!"
I see a man in a yoga pose right at the water's edge. Eyes shut and taking it in.
Another haole man, very sunburnt, grinning, wearing a big sarong.
Two rosy-cheeked grey-haired ladies kissing.

Thoughts

The act of swimming is going into the deep—we cover our body in water, we are the embodiment of the universe – and isn't that just a way of looking for our deeper self in this vast mystery, the ocean, and the universe? We are going deeper to find truth and to find ourselves.

Is this what propels us? The feeling that we are looking at the world in a new way, in a new body, connected to the universe? It is so pleasing and reassuring to be part of this mystery. This idea is embedded in the science of quantum physics—that the universe is in us as we are of the universe. Nowhere do I feel more like this than when I'm in the ocean. We are entangled in the net together.

Cultural anthropologist Margaret Mead once said that she naturally expected to be fortunate and to have consistent good luck. She had bad luck too, but she always got through it by living in her light with the expectation of good fortune. I have been thinking about how fortunate I have been in my life. I have had some misfortune, but the way I have approached this has impacted my life deeply. I have come to recognize how privileged I have been even in my misfortune.

I expect the ocean and the waters to heal me, free me, and awaken me. I honor her and this time with her. She has become my best friend, my therapist, and my *Kapuna* (wise, honored elder). This is what has happened so far. And why I go back in as often as possible.

Aquarius

We are coming closer to moving into the Age of Aquarius once again after many years – and not a minute too soon.

"When the moon is in the Seventh House
And Jupiter aligns with Mars
Then peace will guide the planets
And love will steer the stars
This is the dawning of the age of Aquarius
Age of Aquarius
Aquarius
Aquarius"

-From the musical *Hair* by Ragni, Rado and MacDermot

Kona February 2021

Watching from the shore each day as the colossal humpback whales breech and slap their long pectoral fins against the surface of the water has been astounding. Male humpbacks produce a complex song lasting 10 to 20 minutes, which they repeat for hours at a time. All the males in a group will produce the same song, which is different each season. The whales have no idea what we on land are living through. These huge beasts continue to astonish us, leaping, breaching, blowing, singing their songs for all to hear.

The new American president and his team are on board and all is proceeding in ways that feel safer and sounder, at least to me. Yet, walking on the beach yesterday, I got into a long talk with two Republicans who immigrated here from Eastern Europe a decade ago. We talked for a good hour, and I pledged to listen and to try to find common ground. Trying to go purple! – a bi-partisan blend of red and blue.

I found that I liked them and respected them both, but after a long, civilized conversation we found we could not agree on one single issue or fact, except that we both loved the idea of America and wanted to be good citizens.

I am left with this: to progress and move forward to create a world of equity for every race, gender, and socioeconomic level will be an ongoing struggle that will lurch forward and back with gains and losses. But we must not lose ground even as we change teams. Even as we don't agree on how to progress. Even as we come from different parties. It reminds me of the challenges of creating a theater production, where we build a team consisting of many different people with different backgrounds and views, knowing that if we are to succeed we must all get along and figure out how to accommodate the many viewpoints to make a better show.

Just as when we swim in the ocean, we all get along, having no idea what party we belong to, what school or college we went to, or where we grew up. We just swim together and agree that we are happily blessed and in awe of nature. So, I will keep on trying and keep on swimming until I get it right – or at least do better in accepting our differences.

July 4 2021. Aftermath, Sort Of

We are slowly, cautiously easing out of this horrible global pandemic with a new president, amidst the continuous emergence of new coronavirus variants. Sometimes we wear masks and sometimes we don't. We try to be cautious and brave at the same time. We're inconsistent, just like our government and leaders have been. Because, let's face it, we have never been here before. I am feeling more forgiving as I realize how difficult it all has been. What seems like a clear and obvious scientific decision isn't always well-implemented, doesn't always prove to be the best course. It's a dangerous game of trial and error with the lives of millions at stake, and we humans are the guinea pigs.

Now that the worst is possibly behind us, I don't fully believe this. I am more skeptical, less optimistic. I'm more wary of leaving my cave, my shelter, of being around crowds, of trusting that other humans are acting honorably and safely. I feel extremely vulnerable and recognize that this is a new kind of anxiety for me. Maybe it will pass, maybe not.

The marks of this time are deep—the reckonings of race and gender and economic disparity have all been highlighted in unforgettable ways. We as a nation are traumatized, no matter where you live or what side of the aisle you are on.

So how do we proceed?

I feel that so much new information has been revealed that it's hard to absorb it without feeling deeply distressed.

So much work to be done, so much course-correction needed on our wayward planet. But where do we start? Each day I'm just trying to do better.

I read somewhere that when you are asked to help, you should do it. It's a privilege even to be asked. And it's still more of a privilege to be in a position to help.

Smile at strangers. Say hello. Be concerned.

Let's go retro— back to when the world was more real and less cyber. When we acknowledged one another in person.

No time has been perfect, but small dignities can change someone's day, even yours.

Be Kind. Do Better. Be Generous. I'm going to try.

And keep swimming...

Epilogue

It's Fall 2021

We think we're moving out of this crazy global shut down in some ways, and so today I took a walk along my local beach and was amazed at the many new and old ideas I saw there.

The beach has become a safe outdoor living room for everyone now seeking space and air and no face masks.

Here are a few things I saw today:
- A young man who has figured out the secret to life: A sand-angel
- A Reiki Healer doing Reiki on a patient in the sand.
- A couple married during the time of Covid, celebrating their one-year anniversary together.

More trash than ever pollutes our beaches and our oceans. Man-made toxic pollution kills our fish, destroys habitat, and causes us swimmers and surfers to inhale micro plastics and other harmful toxins as we swim, ultimately polluting and compromising our bodies and our children's bodies.

Can we treat our outdoor living room with the same respect we treat our indoor living rooms? Meaning—don't leave your trash behind. Don't degrade or destroy. Don't pollute. And if we can't do that, consider this—if we don't wake up soon and change our bad habits, we won't have any fish to eat or safe clean water to swim in. A legacy of destroyed beaches and dead eco systems. We are all connected, folks. Please help save the oceans and our largest outdoor living space! We need the ocean and beaches now more than ever! It's up to us and time's up!

As the great, legendary ocean explorer Dr. Sylvia Earle says:

No water, no life
No blue, no green

The end.

In gratitude to my daughter, Alexandra, who encouraged me to do this tiny book, no matter what. Katie, my fabulous right hand—who has the patience of Job and the good humor of a Saint—to this tech dummy boomer. (She says I've gotten better!) Deep thanks to Gayle Scott, editor extraordinaire and almost lifelong friend.

A special thank you to my first open water teacher, Jax Tatro, a real life mermaid; and, to the extraordinary and tireless Karlyn Pipes. To all my fellow swimmers, globally, but especially at Outdoor Swimmer Magazine (outdoorswimmer.com); Swim Feral (swimferal.co.uk); Wild Swimming UK Instagram (Instagram: @wild_swimming_uk), Deakin and Blue bathing suit company, named after Roger Deakin, who changed outdoor swimming in the UK with his iconic book, *Waterlogged*; to Roger MacFarlane nature writer of *Underland* and *The Wild Places*; and to the many books that have inspired me to keep swimming. And, to all of you who have been afraid of the water, but went in any way!

If you are so moved to help our oceans, here are a few organizations that are working hard to keep our oceans safe and clean: Heal the Bay (healthebay.org), The Surfrider Foundation (www.surfrider.org), Pacific Whale Foundation (www.pacificwhale.org), Ocean Foundation (oceanfdn.org), and Surfers Against Sewage (www.sas.org.uk.org).

CPSIA information can be obtained
at www.ICGtesting.com
Printed in the USA
LVHW070826030522
717732LV00009B/290